THE GREAT MASTERS

GEORGE FRIDERIC HANDEL

The Story of his Life and Work

by James S. Hall

BOOSEY AND HAWKES

First edition   1961

Revised and enlarged
         edition   1963

HANDEL'S niche in the Temple of fame rests on a sure foundation. Among famous composers, like a great cricketer, he is essentially the all-rounder. Every kind of music came alike to him from dance rhythms to grand opera. With equal facility he wrote instrumental works, church music and oratorios and it was one of these last, composed when he was fifty-six years old, which he called *Messiah*, which has made his name immortal. To understand his character, and indeed his music, one must follow his life. Handel was one of the first world citizens, who succeeded in being all things to all men. More importantly, he left behind him in every country he visited music of which its citizens may justly be proud.

George Frideric Handel was born in Halle, a town in Saxony, on 23 February 1685. It is of interest that his great contemporary, Johann Sebastian Bach, was born in Eisenach, a town in the same province, less than a month later, on 21 March.

The fact that these two great composers were born so nearly together and lived and worked in the same part of Germany, has led many people to believe that they wrote the same kind of music. Also to raise dispute as to which was the better composer of the two. More careful study will show that there is only a superficial resemblance in the music they wrote, even for the same occasions, and that each of them was a master in his own chosen field. Handel, who had to sell his music at first hearing to fickle audiences, intended that it should have an immediate appeal to the listeners who paid for it. This makes his music more easy to listen to and to understand. Bach, a church organist for most of his life, was not dependent on such things and could and did write deep and thoughtful music to satisfy the spiritual side of his character.

Unlike Bach, our composer came from singularly unmusical stock. His grandfather Valentin Händel was a coppersmith from Breslau, the capital of Silesia, about two hundred and fifty miles from Halle. There are copper mines at Eisleben, quite near to Halle, and Valentin Händel met and married an Eisleben girl, Anne, the daughter of a master coppersmith, Samuel Beichling. A year later he left Breslau, made the long journey to Halle and in March 1609 took the oath as a citizen of the town and made his home there. He was then twenty-six years old. He and Anne had five sons. The two eldest were trained as coppersmiths, the next two died, probably in infancy, and the youngest child, Georg, our composer's father, born in 1622, became a barber. As was usual in those days, he also began to practise surgery.

Georg appears to have done well from the start. When he was barely twenty-one his master died suddenly, leaving his young wife Anna childless, with the business on her hands. She was then thirty-one. It is evident that she put her trust in Georg Händel to carry on the practice and shortly afterwards married him. They had six children, only two of whom, a boy and a girl, survived adolescence.

Georg and Anna prospered and in 1666 they bought a big house in the centre of Halle, only a few minutes' walk from the street where grandfather Valentin started business as a coppersmith. This house, named 'Zum gelben Hirschen' (The Yellow Stag) was originally a wine house and the Händels hoped to continue this profitable business as a side line. Unfortunately they met with great opposition from the local authorities and it was only after a bitter battle lasting three years that Georg obtained his licence from the Elector.

In 1682 Plague broke out in Halle and swept away Gottfried, one of the barber-surgeon's sons, and in the same year his wife Anna died too. Georg Händel decided on immediate re-marriage, probably to obtain a house-keeper for his large establishment, and sought the hand of Dorothea, aged thirty-two, one of the two daughters of his friend Pastor Taust of Giebichenstein, a suburb of Halle. In April 1683 they were married and the following year she had a son, Georg Händel's seventh child, who died at birth.

4

But the eighth, born on 23 February 1685, survived and on the following day was baptized Georg Friederich in the Liebfrauenkirche in the Market Place.

In most families – the Bach family is a notable example – any child with real musical talent would be given opportunity and encouragement. It was not so for young Georg Friederich. Various suggestions have been made by earlier biographers as to how the boy picked up the rudiments of music. These range from his listening to the town bands, choirs and the cathedral services, to practice on an almost noiseless clavichord said to have been smuggled into the attic by his aunt Anna, Dorothea's sister. It is evident that despite his father's antipathy to music as a career for his son, the young Handel found some opportunity for its practice. When he accompanied his father on a visit to Weissenfels, some forty miles from Halle, he managed to obtain access to the organ there and astonished Duke Johann Adolf with his prowess. The Duke at once insisted that such talent must be encouraged and lessons were arranged for the boy, then seven or eight years old, with Friedrich Wilhelm Zachau, the thirty-year-old organist of the Liebfrauenkirche in Halle.

Zachau received both gratitude and affection from his pupil, who was required to produce a church cantata every week. Handel told a friend later that 'he worked like the devil' in those days. It is important to remember that Zachau's chief method of tuition was to set out a musical theme of his own composition, or taken from the works of someone else, around which young Handel had to construct a fresh composition. The fact that he continued this practice in later life has led to many unjust accusations of plagiarism, or stealing other men's ideas. It is possible to show that in many important cases such borrowings were as obvious to Handel's audiences as they were to Zachau. Also, that in Handel's own day they met with no adverse comment.

Three years of hard work with Zachau yielded great results. There exists still a set of six early trios for two oboes and a bass which were shown to Handel many years later. The composer recognized them and remarked that the oboe was then his favourite instrument. These trios exhibit an astonishing maturity for a boy of about ten years old.

In the same period Handel had become an outstanding performer on both organ and harpsichord. It was probably through the influence of the Duke of Saxe-Weissenfels that he was invited to visit Berlin to play before the Elector of Brandenburg. His father consented and the visit was an outstanding success. A further offer by the Elector to complete the boy's musical education in Italy and then to give him a position at the Berlin Court was refused. So Handel returned to Halle, where after five years of schooling in the Lutheran Gymnasium he matriculated in February 1702. It was shortly after his return from Berlin that his father died at the age of seventy-five.

That Handel managed to find time for music in between his studies is evident from his friendship with Georg Philipp Telemann (1681–1767), a rising young composer, living in Leipzig and reluctantly committed to the study of law. In 1701 we find Telemann knew all about the 'already accomplished Georg Friedrich Händel'. This is important, not only in dating the beginning of a life-long friendship between these composers, for it gives us a vital clue as to where and how Handel obtained his experience of Italian opera and the urge to write it. Telemann had already acquired considerable aptitude in this medium. There was then no opera house in Halle but quite a number of operas were staged at the Ducal court at Weissenfels. It is significant that young Telemann wrote four of them. Most of these operas were sung in a barbarous mixture of German and Italian and we have to account for the fact that by 1704 Handel was writing better operas fluently in both languages. Telemann found Handel an unsettling

companion for his law studies and spoke of 'nearly im-
bibing music poison from him.' In the event, both young
men abandoned their law careers and it seems probable
that the dose of 'music-poison' indicates much closer
co-operation between them in the Weissenfels operas than
has been recorded in past history.

Shortly after Handel entered Halle University in 1702
he was offered, and accepted, a twelve months' contract
as organist to the large Calvinist Domkirche in Halle.
Several authorities tell us that Handel was intensely busy
with choral music and the training of church choirs during
this period. No doubt he was, though the evidence is
conflicting. It makes better sense if we regard this period
as a year of decision in which this young man of eighteen
finally made up his mind that neither the legal profession,
nor life in Halle as a church organist could fulfil his destiny.
It is, however, interesting that the one composition we
can with some authenticity relate to this period is a setting
of the psalm *Laudate Pueri* in Latin which is more suitable
for use in Vespers in a Roman Catholic Church.

In the early summer of 1703 Handel took leave of his family
and of Halle. As far as we know, friendless and alone he made
his way to Hamburg two hundred miles away. This was the
first of many such long journeys in which the composer took
his courage in both hands, trusting his future solely to his
faith in himself or to the guiding hand of Providence.

We know that he borrowed some money from his
mother for the Hamburg journey, but as a widow her
means must have been limited and the fact that the loan
was soon repaid shows that the amount was a small one.

Hamburg was a free city and a magnet for artists and
musicians from all over Europe. It had a flourishing opera
house, built twenty-five years earlier in which performances
were given in French, German and Italian. By 1703 Italian
airs were sweeping the board and the city had become a
centre of pomp and extravagance. It was a strange place
for a youth of eighteen to begin his musical career.

* * *

Handel's first thought was to find himself a job. He went to the opera house, then under the direction of a twenty-nine year old composer named Reinhard Keiser who himself had been born near Weissenfels. There is no present evidence of a significant link, though the two men, in the limited field of grand opera, must have had common contacts. Keiser was an extraordinary character who combined a life of extravagance and dissipation with a tremendous capacity for work. He had considerable musical talent and the gift of melody. In his Hamburg life alone he composed a hundred and twenty operas, partly or wholly in Italian. His formative influence on Handel was considerable for we find many traces of his themes and operatic style in later Handelian works. More importantly, he promptly found Handel a job, at first a humble one, among the second violins in the opera orchestra.

Here Handel made one of the most important contacts of his life, a composer and singer named Johann Mattheson, four years older than himself. Later, in his memoirs, Mattheson wrote: 'Handel came to Hamburg in the summer of 1703, rich only in ability and goodwill. I was almost the first with whom he made acquaintance. I took him round to all the choirs and organs here, and introduced him to operas and concerts, particularly to a certain house where everything was given up to music. At first he played second violin in the opera orchestra and behaved as if he could not count up to five, being naturally inclined to a dry humour. (I know well enough that he will laugh heartily when he reads this, though as a rule he laughs but little). Especially if he remembers the pigeon fancier, who travelled with us by the post to Lübeck, or Becker, the pastrycook's son who blew the bellows for us when we played at the Maria Magdalena Church there. That was on 30 July and on 15 July we had been for a water party.'

Handel's visit to Lübeck, which is about forty miles north-east of Hamburg, was to accompany his friend who was a candidate for the post of organist in place of the famous Buxtehude who was retiring. But finding that the post also involved a marriage with Buxtehude's daughter, a lady some twelve years older than themselves, the young men tactfully declined the position and returned to Hamburg.

A little later when the regular harpsichord player in the Hamburg opera house failed to appear, Handel in the emergency took his place and astonished the orchestra with his prowess – a fact which Mattheson records was till then known only to himself. This led shortly afterwards to a serious quarrel between the two friends in which Handel nearly lost his life. Mattheson tells the story which occurred during his own opera *Cleopatra*, in which Handel played the harpsichord and Mattheson himself sang the principal tenor part.

'I as composer directed the performance and also sang the part of Antony, who has to die a good half-hour before the end of the opera. Hitherto I had been accustomed after finishing my part to go into the orchestra and accompany the remaining scenes, and this is a thing which incontestably the composer can do better than any one else. However, on this occasion Handel refused to give up his place. On this account we were incited by some who were present to engage in a duel in the open market place, after the performance was over, before a crowd of spectators – a piece of folly which might have turned out disastrously for both of us, had not my blade splintered by God's grace upon a broad metal button on Handel's coat. No harm came of the encounter and we were soon reconciled again by the kind influences of a worthy councillor and the manager of the theatre. Whereupon I entertained Handel at dinner on that very day, the 30th of December, after which we went together to the rehearsal of his opera *Almira*, and were better friends than ever.'

Almira, Handel's first venture in the operatic field, was a strange bi-lingual concoction based on episodes in the life of Almira, Queen of Castile, with the sub-title 'The Vicissitudes of Royalty'. The recitatives and some of the airs are set to German words by Friedrich Feustking, a librettist of little worth, but fourteen songs were left in their original Italian, taken from an earlier play by Lopez de Vega. The freshness and vigour of the music brought Handel immediate success and the opera ran for twenty performances or more. Percy Robinson[1] believed that quite a number of its themes were used by J. S. Bach when, twenty years later, he wrote his great *St Matthew Passion*. This success was in contrast with the lukewarm reception given to Handel's setting of the *St John Passion* earlier in the same year.

Fired by the success of *Almira*, Handel obtained another libretto from Feustking and plunged into the composition of *Nero*, or *Love obtained through Blood and Murder*. Despite its arresting title, this opera was a failure, having only three performances. Unfortunately the music is now lost.

With his desire to earn money Handel found Mattheson's earlier introduction of great help. Mattheson wrote: 'I introduced him ... to many houses where he played music, which procured him many pupils.' Among these was Cyril Wyche, the son of John Wyche, the British Resident at Hamburg from 1702–13. John Wyche was the son of Sir Peter Wyche, formerly envoy at the Court of Muscovy, prior to his transfer to the Residency at Hamburg. The Wyche family was related to the Granvilles in England, several members of whom became Handel's greatest friends and patrons. There is no doubt that this introduction to the Wyche household was Handel's first firm contact with the British aristocracy and it shows us his wonderful gift for making lasting friends in high places. It is not too much to say that his first step over the Wyche doorstep was the one on the long road which led him to a lifetime of honour and prosperity in England and to a tomb and monument in Westminster Abbey more than half a century afterwards.

Handel's pupils proved profitable and during the next

eighteen months he was able to repay his mother's loan and make plans for his long hoped for journey to Italy. His first biographer, Mainwaring,[2] quaintly remarks: 'For he resolved to go to Italy on his own bottom, as soon as he could make a purse for that occasion'. He achieved this by the summer of 1706 and in addition made an influential friend with his operatic music. This was Giovanni Gastone, the impecunious second son of the Grand Duke of Tuscany, whose court was at Pratolino, a few miles from Florence. Giangastone, as he was generally called, was a deplorable character but he was able to give Handel a very valuable introduction to his father and his brother Ferdinand de'Medici as a start to the composer's visit to Italy.

Handel found time, before he left Hamburg, to write another opera called *Florindo und Daphne* but this was not performed until 1708, long after his departure. Owing to its great length it was divided into two parts which were performed separately with two new titles in German. These mean approximately 'Happy Florindo' and 'Transformed Daphne'. The music is lost and only two known copies of the libretto still exist.

*   *   *

The Italian journey probably began with a visit to Halle in the late summer of 1706. Handel retained a great affection for his mother all his life and certainly missed no reasonable opportunity of visiting her. Mainwaring tells us that he had made up a purse of two hundred ducats (this has been estimated to be about £96) and Mattheson said that he had a free journey to Italy with one 'von Binitz'. No other proof exists of this but we have Mattheson's own evidence that Handel was an entertaining travelling companion.

Florence was his first goal and he arrived there in the autumn of 1706, probably with the libretto of his next opera *Rodrigo* in his pocket. Although the work was produced with considerable success, the orchestra seems to have been inadequate. Further disappointment awaited him in Rome, where a complete ban existed against the performance of operas. This destroyed any hopes which Handel may have had of writing operas for Rome. We must also remember that Rome was very much in the grip of the Roman Catholic Church who could hardly be expected to have any liking for heretics, either Lutheran or otherwise.

Recent research[3] offers us at least a logical explanation for Handel's success in Rome, despite all attempts to convert him to the Catholic Faith. Briefly its assumes, on fair evidence, that while in Florence, where his welcome as a composer of operas and secular cantatas was assured, Cardinal Carlo Colonna, or one of his emissaries, commissioned him to write a magnificent set of *Vespers of the Blessed Virgin*.

We can date Handel's arrival in Rome from an entry in the *Valesio* Diary of 14 January 1707, whose discovery we owe to Sir Newman Flower:[4] 'There has arrived in this city a Saxon, an excellent player on the cembalo (harpsichord) and a composer of music, who has to-day displayed his ability in playing the organ in the Church of St John (Lateran) to the amazement of everyone'. It is evident that Handel's technical skill as a performer won him immediate recognition. This has satisfied all his biographers, but they have not faced the problem of how he got into the church of St John Lateran in the first place. This is the Pope's own Cathedral, as Bishop of Rome, and the last place in which one would expect to find a young Lutheran composer, a professed heretic in the eyes of the Roman Church. Mainwaring indeed tells us that 'his persuasion was so totally repugnant to theirs that many unsuccessful attempts were made to lead him out of the road to damnation.'

Musically, however, Handel was prepared to be all things to all men. With Cardinal Colonna as his firm sponsor and a promise of fine Church music to come, many evident obstacles to his career were cleared away.

While opera was banned, both religious and chamber music enjoyed a great vogue in Rome and regular musical soirées were held in the palaces of the cardinals and members of the Roman aristocracy. At these Handel became a welcome guest, notably of Prince Ruspoli, Cardinal Ottoboni and Cardinal Pamfili. This last cardinal provided him with the text of an allegorical cantata *Il trionfo del tempo*.

The great centre of Rome's social and musical life was known as the Academy of the Arcadians which met together at Prince Ruspoli's palace, or rather in its gardens on the Esquilino. Handel was only twenty-two years old and not eligible for membership as the Academy had an age limit of twenty-four. But his harpsichord playing and fluent gift for composing cantatas made him an ever welcome guest. Here he soon found himself on terms of intimacy with great composers like the Scarlattis, Corelli and others, who did so much later to help his musical career. This Academy was a spiritual brotherhood of poets, authors and musicians. The members called themselves 'shepherds' and took such classical names as Terpandro, Archimelo and Protico. Among these 'shepherds' were counted four Popes (Clement XI, Innocent XIII, Clement XII and Benedict XIII). It was no doubt through this powerful gathering that Handel made the acquaintance of Cardinal Grimani, the Viceroy of Naples, who later wrote for him the libretto of the opera *Agrippina*. This was the most successful of all his Italian works when it was performed in Venice two years later.

Domenico Scarlatti, an outstanding exponent of the harpsichord, is said to have had many friendly contests with the young Handel with undecided results. But for organ playing Scarlatti was the first to declare Handel the victor. It is also on record that whenever Scarlatti heard Handel's name mentioned he made the sign of the Cross.

Handel's magnificent set of Vespers was sung on 16 July 1707 in the Carmelite Church of Santa Maria di Monte Santo and after that all doors were open to him.[5] It is probable that he received and accepted invitations to visit houses and religious foundations in northern Italy and that he often repaid periods of brief hospitality with short musical compositions. A small number of disconnected motets and cantatas, referable to this period, are still being found and published. Two Latin motets, *Coelestis dum spirat* and *O qualis de coelo* are eminently suitable for 12 and 13 June 1707, especially if they were sung in the church of St Anthony in Padua, to which saint the first motet is dedicated. There has also been an interesting controversy about the 'Erba' *Magnificat* and the 'Urio' *Te Deum,* one side suggesting that Handel composed them while staying at these towns near Lake Como, while the other insists that he just used the music by two lesser composers of the same name. Much of it was revived by him thirty years later in *Israel in Egypt* and the *Dettingen Te Deum.*

*   *   *

Handel certainly visited Florence again in the autumn of 1707 and several biographers believe that the production of his opera *Rodrigo* should be referred to this date. There is an often repeated story that the heroine of *Rodrigo,* one Vittoria Tesi, fell madly in love with Handel and later pursued him to Venice. Unfortunately for romance this brilliant and beautiful contralto was only seven years old at the time and the biographers have omitted to notice that *Rodrigo* contains no female contralto part. There was a Vittoria Tarquini, known as La Bombace, who sang in *Rodrigo* but she was reputedly both old and ugly so that we may regard this story as another fable. With it goes another that Prince Ferdinand gave Handel a hundred sequins, together with a porcelain (or silver) dinner service in return for his opera. But, as William C. Smith[6] dryly remarks, it was surely a strange gift to a young man of twenty-two or so, who had no establishment of his own and was likely to be moving about.

We know that Handel was in Rome in March and April 1708 and that he stayed at Prince Ruspoli's palace for the archives still contain the entries: 'Paid for the carriage of the bed and other things for Monsù. Endel 10 bajocci (about fivepence)' and 'Paid to the Jew for hire of the said bed and counterpanes for one month 70 bajocci'. (2s 11d). In return Prince Ruspoli received the oratorio *La Resurrezione* which was given on Easter Sunday 8 April, in the Bonelli Palace with the famous Corelli leading an orchestra of at least forty players. The oratorio was an immediate success though next day the Pope issued a public reproof because a female singer took part in it.

Shortly afterwards Handel set Cardinal Pamfili's *Il Trionfo del Tempo* to music but some describe it as a failure.

Either the poor reception of *Il Trionfo,* or the imminent threat of invasion of Rome by an army from the North, may have induced Handel to travel south to Naples in May or June 1708. Here, for the wedding of the Duke of Alvito he wrote the serenata *Aci Galatea e Polifemo,* the manuscript of which is helpfully signed and dated at Naples on 16 June. It is recorded that he wrote this work to please a Spanish Princess named Donna Laura, with whom some say he had quite a serious love affair.

Another versatile effort in Naples was his set of seven French canzonets written in the style of Lully. These were, no doubt, a small thank-offering for hospitality received. We have no clear evidence about the composer's movements for the next twelve months, but it is tempting to believe that he spent the winter of 1708 and the early part of 1709 staying with his new friends in Southern Italy. Indeed Mainwaring says: 'While he was at Naples he received invitations from most of the principal persons who lived within reach of that capital; and lucky was he esteemed, who could engage him soonest, and detain him longest.'

Although most biographers say that he returned to Rome a third time in 1709, it is more probable that it was only as a stage in his journey north to Venice. We have no reason to believe that he stayed in Rome and it is more likely that the summer of 1709 was spent visiting some of the towns in northern Italy to which reference has already been made. He certainly arrived in Venice before December 1709 and commenced preparations for his opera *Agrippina*. The first performance on 26 December drew cries from the audience of 'Viva il caro Sassone' (Long live the dear Saxon) and the opera filled Cardinal Grimani's Venetian Theatre for twenty-seven nights. Among the audience were Prince Ernst Augustus of Hanover, younger brother of the Elector, later George I. With him was Baron Kielmansegg, a prominent equerry at the same Court, and Charles, 4th Earl of Manchester, Ambassador to the Republic of Venice. All three are thought to have played an important part in inviting Handel to visit Hanover and England and in their respective spheres were responsible for the warm welcome he received there.

Among the singers in *Agrippina* was the famous castrato Valeriano Pellegrini, who was employed at the court of the Elector Palatine, Boschi, a tremendous bass with a compass of two octaves and a half, may have sung bass in *La Resurrezione*. Handel, characteristically, wrote him songs in both oratorio and opera containing double octave leaps beyond the capacity of any normal singer. The part of the Empress Agrippina was given to Francesca Durastanti, who may have been the soprano who had incurred the Pope's displeasure in *La Resurrezione*. There is an interesting musical clue to suggest this. To illustrate Mary Magdalen's joy at the Resurrection, she was given a light-hearted little song 'Ho un non so che nel cor' with a simple violin and violoncello accompaniment. Perhaps the levity of this song also upset the Pope but certainly not Handel, who gave the song unaltered to the Empress Agrippina. Signora Boschi also was evidently captivated by the air, made it her own

A coloured 18th century portrait of George Frideric Handel

View of **VAUX-HALL** *Gardens.*

– from engraving of 1790

property and took it to England, where, some months before Handel's arrival there she introduced it into her part in Alessandro Scarlatti's opera *Pirro e Demetrio*.[7]

Handel left Italy in the spring of 1710, probably as soon as the mountain roads were clear and very probably in the company of Baron Kielmansegg, for he went directly to the Hanoverian Court. Here he was welcomed by Steffani, the Director of Music and the Elector himself who offered Handel the substantial salary of 1,000 thalers (approximately £300) to join his service. Handel accepted the offer with the proviso that he had already promised to pay a visit to the Elector Palatine at Dusseldorf and to visit England. He was generously given twelve months' leave to fulfil these engagements. In addition Steffani voluntarily resigned his post at the Court in Handel's favour.

During Handel's absence in Italy, his younger sister Johanna had died in July 1709 and no doubt he made a visit to his mother at Halle, a hundred and fifty miles away, a matter for priority. It is less clear whether such a visit was made before or after his Court appointment in June 1710. We have four clear months to cover his visit to Dusseldorf and his journey through Holland to England which he reached in the late autumn.

Possibly the first thing he heard whistled in the streets of London was Mary Magdalen's little song from *La Resurrezione*, whose catchy little air, set to less seemly English words, had become a popular ballad.

* * *

Handel has been accused of the murder of English music. The injustice of this accusation is evident after fair appraisal of the position in 1710. With the passing of Henry Purcell, fifteen years before, followed by John Blow, native English music was as good as dead. Our next composers of merit, such as Arne and Boyce, were still in their cradles. Operatic music in particular was at its lowest ebb, despite a growing demand for it, especially the Italian variety. Handel's fame had preceded him and his visit aroused both interest and expectation. Although several biographers speak of his introduction to Queen Anne and her Court, it is more probable that he went first to the director of the opera, Aaron Hill.

Aaron Hill promptly suggested that Handel should collaborate with him in the production of an opera. This was to be based on the tale of Rinaldo and Armida, and the liberation of Jerusalem from the Saracens. As popular taste demanded that the opera be sung in Italian, Aaron Hill's libretto was given to an itinerant writer named Giacomo Rossi to be set in that language. As fast as Rossi wrote his verses Handel provided the music, at times outstripping the Italian who complained that the composer was frequently ahead of him. Between them, the opera was finished in a fortnight and was presented at the Queen's Theatre in the Haymarket on 24 February 1711. It had a tremendous reception for its fifteen performances.

Public demand for printed copies of *Rinaldo* brought Handel into contact with John Walsh, a leading music publisher. Within a few months he sold out successive editions of the overture and favourite songs. There is the often-told story that Walsh made a profit of £1,500 from the sale of this work and that Handel wryly remarked: 'My dear Sir, next time you shall compose the opera and I will sell it'. But the amount cannot be true.

That Handel had some serious disagreement with the publisher is probable. John Walsh, father and son, eventually obtained a monopoly to print and publish all Handel's works, but it was not till 1722, over ten years afterwards, that they were given another Handel score. Some biographers give us the impression that Handel was exploited by these unscrupulous publishers. There is real evidence to suggest that both parties were shrewd business men and unyielding in matters of principle.

Rinaldo brought Handel patronage from the great.

18

Heidegger, a famous operatic manager and reputedly the ugliest man in Europe, introduced him to the Granville family. Here he met Mary Granville, aged eleven. We know her better as Mrs Delany. He played on her little spinet and started a lifetime's friendship. He also became very friendly with the Burlington family who seem to have adopted him. Dent[8] tells us that Lady Burlington introduced him to Queen Anne and that her son, Lord Burlington offered him prolonged hospitality.

Another humble but important contact was with Thomas Britton, a small coal man. He carried his sacks of coal by day and ran a musical club by night. It had become fashionable for Society and the artistic professions to meet in his long low loft above the coal store, climbing a flight of rickety stairs to get there. Here Handel played the little chamber organ and met fellow musicians like Pepusch, together with many influential amateurs on friendly terms.

Rinaldo finished its run on 2 June and shortly afterwards Handel returned to his obligations in Hanover with a brief visit to the Elector Palatine at Dusseldorf on the way. It is significant that this worthy wrote separate letters for Handel to take to the Elector and dowager Electress of Hanover to excuse some delay in his return. Once back at Hanover, Handel soon regained favour, writing a number of songs and a set of chamber duets for Princess Caroline of Anspach, always his good friend and patron. We meet her later as the unhappy wife of George II.

In the later autumn Handel re-visited Halle and on 23 November stood as godfather to the daughter of his last surviving sister, Dorothea Michaelsen, who had married a lawyer from Hamburg in 1708. The baby was named Johanna Friderica – the second name, of course, in the composer's honour. Handel became very fond of his little niece and later left her the bulk of his fortune. Then back he went to the Court at Hanover for nearly a year. He found time to study English and to write letters to his friends in England. One such letter probably induced

John Hughes, the poet, to provide him with an English Cantata, *Venus and Adonis*. Two of the arias, 'Dear Adonis' and 'Transporting Joy' still exist – our first example of Handel setting music to English words. They were discovered in quite recent years among the music manuscripts in the British Museum by William C. Smith.

He also made a start on his next opera *Il Pastor Fido* to a text again by Rossi and evidently intended for the English stage. The Elector again granted him leave of absence, it is said for a strictly limited stay in England where he arrived about the end of October 1712. His new opera was completed on 24 October and went on at the opera house in the Haymarket exactly a month later. It had only seven performances. Francis Colman[9] wrote that it was short and that the characters wore old clothes. Probably Handel only intended it to be a stop-gap before his next opera *Teseo*, a much grander affair, which he finished on 19 December. This was performed less than a month later on 10 January. The speed of production of these Handel operas is startling when one considers their complex and often lavish scenery, the scanty rehearsal time and the fact that all the music was in manuscript, the parts copied out singly by hand.

Teseo was a greater success than *Il Pastor Fido* and had thirteen performances. Unfortunately for Handel, his manager, Owen MacSwiney, was a rascal and absconded with the receipts from the first two houses, both full to capacity. The ugly 'Swiss Count' Heidegger came to the rescue and took over the production of the remaining performances but the net financial gains must have been small. To make up for this the run ended with a special performance 'For the benefit of Mr Hendel'.

For some of this period Handel stayed with a Mr Andrews at Barn Elms, a house on the Surrey bank of the Thames, though during the performances of *Teseo* he accepted the hospitality of Lord Burlington who had a fine mansion in Piccadilly. He is said by some to have lived there for the next three years. But the possibility that his Hanover appointment had been terminated during the previous year deserves consideration. The commonly accepted story about his truancy involves a slur on the honour of a man whose whole life was characterized by personal integrity. The evidence deserves some critical re-examination. Mainwaring himself tells us that Queen Anne gave Handel a pension of £200 – a curious thing to do if he was still in someone else's employment.

Then there is the negative evidence that we can find no trace of the embittered correspondence between Hanover and London which we might have some right to expect, nor any reference whatever to Handel occupying a false position. In 1711 Walsh published seven editions of *Rinaldo* or its instrumental parts. The first, on 24 April just says 'Compos'd by Mr Hendel'. The second and third, put out about May-June, describe him as 'Maestro di Capella' and 'Chapple Master' to the Elector of Hanover. Two editions, which are flute arrangements from the score, bear no author's name. It is true that between 1714 and 1726 Walsh re-issued the second edition, with only minor alterations, from the original plates and with the same title page. The chief purpose of these re-issues was to add English words 'Let ye Waiter bring clean Glasses' to the popular Italian song 'Il tricerbero humiliato'. But it is also clear that the reprint of Handel's out-dated title was due to laziness or economy on Walsh's part. From August 1714 the Elector of Hanover became George I of England. His early relations with Handel, which re-enforce the above argument, are described a little later, after his accession.

*　　*　　*

Meanwhile, Handel was consolidating his position at the English Court. Shrewdly anticipating the Peace of Utrecht, he composed in January 1713 a solemn *Te Deum* and *Jubilate*, ignoring the fact that the Elector would regard such a treaty with extreme distaste and followed it with a fine Ode in honour of Queen Anne's birthday which fell on 6 February. The *Utrecht Te Deum* and *Jubilate*, carefully written in the English style, after the manner of Purcell, were solemnly performed on 7 July 1713 at St Paul's Cathedral. Most authorities, including Chrysander, attribute the Birthday Ode to 1713 as well and it is tempting to believe than Handel, always an opportunist, had to some extent to supplant John Eccles, the Court composer, to get his *Te Deum* sung. John Eccles had written a similar Ode in 1707, no doubt repeated at annual intervals. But more recently, William C. Smith has produced a number of facts to show that this Ode, which contains a definite reference to the Peace of Utrecht, was belatedly performed at a Ball and Entertainment at Windsor on 6 February 1714. Either in 1713 or 1714 Queen Anne is said to have rewarded Handel with a pension of £200.

On Sunday, 1 August 1714 Queen Anne died and the succession passed to the Elector of Hanover. He landed in England on 18 September to be crowned as George I on 20 October. His first official function was to visit the Royal Chapel at St James on 26 September to attend a Service of Thanksgiving and to hear 'A *Te Deum* . . . composed by Mr Handel'. One doubts whether Handel would have served up the *Utrecht Te Deum*, with its unpopular associations, but there exists a *Te Deum in D major* which Chrysander, on general grounds, refers to 1714. In any case, it would have been tactful for him to write a new one.

The newly crowned king did not attend a revival of *Arminio* at the Haymarket theatre on 23 October, but the Prince and Princess of Wales, George and Caroline, did. In Caroline, Handel had a loyal patron till her death – which Dr Raymond Heirons has shown to be due to an abdominal emergency[10] – in 1737. The King, however, attended a command performance of *Rinaldo* on 30 December and another command performance of Handel's new opera *Amadigi* on 16 May in the following year. The

22

picture resolves into that of a King glad and anxious to hear and encourage Handel's music, though probably not on cordial relations with the composer himself. The reasons for this should be sufficiently evident from the facts we have just reviewed.

Fortunately Handel had two other staunch friends at Court, Baron Kielmansegg and Francesco Geminiani, a composer and distinguished violinist who came to England in 1714. It is thought that at this time Handel received a further pension of £200 in addition to the continuance of the one given to him by Queen Anne.

Certainly in a note dated March 1715, he refers to a holding of £500 of South Sea Stock, so he was obviously able to save money, even in the early days. Handel was always prudent in money matters and although some ventures lost money, the stories of his bankruptcies are entirely false. Indeed, the discovery of Handel's private account in the Bank of England, by Dr Percy Young, shows that even in his worst years there was always a substantial balance in hand.[11]

Water parties on the Thames to Richmond or to Hampton Court were a popular Court pastime and gave Handel an opportunity to please the King by composing special music which his band played on a following barge. The actual dates of these are uncertain, except for a known occasion on Wednesday, 17 July 1717 when Handel and about fifty musicians followed the King's party from Whitehall to Chelsea at 8 o'clock in the evening. It is quite probable that there were earlier and later occasions.

As evidence we note with interest that recent evaluation of the *Water Music* suggests that the full twenty movements are a compilation of at least two and possibly three sets of Water Music.

Jacobite alarms and local riots closed the opera houses in London early in 1717, but *Amadigi* was revived in June. On 7 July the King left England for a visit to Hanover, Handel following him shortly afterwards. After a short stay in Halle the composer spent some time in Anspach, where he met Johann Christoph Schmidt, who later, as John Christopher Smith, became his lifetime friend and secretary. Schmidt, who was in the wool trade, had personal reasons for leaving Anspach as well as a devotion to music. He accepted an invitation to come to England and by 1719 was installed in a house in Dean Street, Soho, his wife and three children following him later.[12]

Handel's only composition in 1716 appears to have been a fine setting of the St Matthew Passion by Brockes of Hamburg. Returning to London, Handel arranged fresh performances of *Amadagi* and *Rinaldo* for the 1717 season and enlivened them by the introduction of dancers. In another company at the theatre was a young French girl, Marie Sallé, then only about ten years old. She made so evident an impression on Handel that many years later, in 1734 and 1735, he invited her to join his cast and wrote special ballet music for her into the operas he produced at that time. Handel's dance music, especially his minuets, became very popular. They were probably first written for the Court and many were re-set as love songs to English words, with or without his permission.

It was in 1717 that James Brydges, later Duke of Chandos, who had amassed a fortune as Paymaster-General in Queen Anne's army, decided that he needed the personal services of the now famous composer Handel. At that time Dr Pepusch was installed as Master of Music in the Duke's palatial mansion at Cannons, near Edgware. Although Handel wrote and no doubt performed a good deal of music for the Duke during the next three years, he did not supplant Pepusch, for we find this worthy signing an inventory of music at Cannons in August 1720. Nor is there any firm evidence that Handel actually lived at Cannons, though the journey to and from London, on a road infested by highwaymen, was known to be a perilous one. Handel composed for the Duke at least eleven fine anthems and a Te Deum (the *Chandos Anthems* and *Chandos*

24

Te Deum), together with the masques of *Acis and Galatea* and *Hamon and Mordecai* which was later re-written and called *Esther*.

*   *   *

In 1719 Handel returned to opera. This was made possible by a body of the nobility, headed by the Duke of Newcastle, who launched a venture called the Royal Academy of Music. It attracted sixty-two subscribers who jointly guaranteed a sum of £50,000 and George I promised to give £1,000 annually for seven years. Handel was to be the principal composer though Giovanni Bononcini and Attilio Ariosti were engaged later on. We may note here that for the next twenty years, Handel's personal fortune largely depended on the success of the music, chiefly operatic, which he wrote for a limited audience composed of the aristocracy and their personal friends. They wanted good Italian opera and were prepared to pay for it.

He began with a visit to the opera house at Dresden, authorized to engage the best soloists almost regardless of price. These included Senesino, the most famous castrato of the age, together with his old friends Boschi and Signora Durastanti, whose figure by now was causing adverse comment. Benedetto Baldassari, a castrato soprano, was picked up at Dusseldorf. This business concluded, he went on to Halle to see his mother. Their reunion was saddened by the death of Dorothea Sophia, his last surviving sister, in August, the previous year. J. S. Bach, hearing that Handel was in Halle, courteously made the journey of twenty-five miles from Cöthen to meet him. But their one opportunity of meeting was lost, for Handel had left for England the day before.

Soon after his return, probably in December 1719, he began the composition of the fine opera *Il Radamisto*, to be performed as his special piece for the Royal Academy on 27 April 1720 with great success. Mainwaring described the crowd: 'Many, who had forced their way into the house with an impetuosity but ill suited to their rank and sex, actually fainted through the excessive heat and closeness of it. Several gentlemen were turned back, who had offered forty shillings for a seat in the gallery, after having despaired of getting any in the pit or boxes'.

In June 1720, George I granted the composer a fourteen-year Privilege to print and publish his works. Handel promptly engaged Richard Meares to publish *Radamisto* and a volume of eight *Suites* for the harpsichord, both finely engraved. The composer complains in a dedication leaf that he was obliged to publish his volume of *Suites* 'because surrepticious and incorrect Copies of them had got Abroad'. All volumes contained the Royal Privilege leaf and were advertised for sale by Christopher Smith, now installed as a music publisher, at the Hand and Music book shop in Coventry Street. The *Suites* contain the piece (No. 5, in E major) now known as the 'Harmonious Blacksmith'. This title first appeared more than fifty years after the composer's death, to the detriment of the usually accepted story about the musical anvil. Nor is it likely that the *Suites* were written for the three young Princesses. Handel was officially appointed their music master eight years later when it is believed that another pension of £200 came his way.

The Directors next invited their three composers to write an opera called *Muzio Scaevola*, each to provide one act with its overture. Handel wrote the third, incompletely published, this time by Meares and John Walsh in two separate editions. Walsh is said to have paid Handel £72 for the score of *Floridante*. This opera, produced in December 1721 had fifteen performances, thanks to the arrival of Senesino who despite his vanity and arrogance became the idol of the ladies in the audience.

It was in December 1723 that Handel took up his permanent residence in a new house in Mayfair (now 25 Brook Street). Meanwhile, with the Academy's consent he engaged a new and famous soprano, Signora Cuzzoni, authorizing the messenger he sent to Italy to offer her £2,000 a year if necessary. Despite her perfect voice, she gave Handel a lot of trouble. It is related that while rehearsing for *Ottone* she flatly refused to sing the fine song 'Falsa imagine' which Handel had written for her. He lost his temper, picked her up and took her to an open window, threatening to throw her out. 'Madam' he said, 'I know that you are a veritable she-devil but I am Beelzebub, chief of the devils'.

In the next opera, *Flavio*, Handel again had trouble. But this time it was with John Gordon, an English tenor, who said that he would jump on Handel's harpsichord and break it if he continued to accompany him in such a manner. 'Good', said Handel, 'I will advertise it, for more people will come to see you jump than to hear you sing'. Study of Gordon's one song shows that the singer obviously wished to introduce a cadenza, a luxury which Handel only allowed to his favourites.

A revival of *Ottone* was followed by *Giulio Cesare*, a sumptuously scored opera with four horn parts, then a novelty. This was a still greater success but with success came jealousy. Open rivalry between Handel and Bononcini was fostered by a section of the nobility. Bononcini's contract with the Academy was terminated but the Duchess of Marlborough offered him £500 a year to stay in England. Handel also seems to have broken off his relations with John Walsh, for his next eight operas, together with *Giulio Cesare* were published by John Cluer in association with Bezaleel Creake and Christopher Smith.

During the next two years Handel gave the Academy *Tamerlano, Rodelinda* and *Scipio*. Cuzzoni and Senesino starred in all three, and it is related that in *Rodelinda* Cuzzoni's brown and silver dress caused more sensation than Handel's music.

After a solitary profit of 7 per cent in the 1723 season, the Academy ran increasingly into debt. Many calls of 5 per cent were made on its subscribers. So in 1725 attempts were made to attract a young and famous singer, Faustina Bordoni, from Vienna. She asked for £2,500 a year and this sum may actually have been paid. By the time she arrived, early in 1726, fifteen calls had been made on the subscribers to the Academy. Although Faustina provided London with a new sensation, it put Handel in a most unenviable position. Cuzzoni, naturally jealous of a young and attractive rival and the high salary which she demanded, was in no mood to welcome her among the cast.

But Handel rose to the occasion. During the next three years he composed the operas *Alessandro, Admeto, Riccardo Primo, Siroe* and *Tolomeo*. Writing for his difficult pair of prima donnas was made no easier by the inclusion of the temperamental Senesino. But he managed to balance their parts to a hair's-breadth.

Rival factions supported each singer and in 1727 disgraceful scenes occurred in the opera house as Cuzzoni and Faustina were alternately applauded and hissed by their individual supporters. The climax came during a performance of Bononcini's opera *Astyanax* in the presence of the Princess of Wales, when, goaded beyond endurance, the two singers fought on the stage. By 1728 the Academy was almost bankrupt so Faustina's illness in June was made the occasion for closing down the opera season. After this the three star singers returned to Italy, leaving the Haymarket theatre deserted for the following year.

Earlier, in 1727, Handel, probably wishing to consolidate his position as composer to the Court, applied for naturalization papers as a British subject. Assent was granted and on 14 February 1727 Handel took the oath of Allegiance and Supremacy. On 20 February, the King's consent made him a British subject.

It was a far-sighted move and proved so when on 11 June 1727 George I died at Osnabrück and his forty-year-old son was proclaimed George II. The new King confirmed Handel in the honorary title of Composer of

Musick to the Chapel Royal and also made him Composer to the Court. He had already been appointed music teacher to the three Royal Princesses and from 1728, at least, received his further pension of £200 for this service. One of his first tasks for the new King was to write a magnificent set of four *Coronation Anthems* for performance at the ceremony in Westminster Abbey on 11 October. It is a tribute to his choice that the first anthem *Zadok the Priest* has been used at the coronation of every British monarch ever since.

Another factor which contributed to the downfall of the Academy was the success of the *Beggar's Opera*. This was a bawdy satire with words by Gay, arranged to popular tunes by Pepusch. Among them were some by Handel himself. It was produced by John Rich at the theatre in Lincoln's Inn Fields and won the slogan that it 'made Gay rich and Rich gay'.

* * *

Contemporary letters show us that relations between Handel, Cuzzoni and Senesino had already reached breaking point. So in January 1729 the composer left for Italy to engage a new cast of singers, with the firm promise of support by former Academy members if their names were satisfactory. We may note here that despite the dead loss of the first venture, the individual subscribers had for the past nine years received in return their seats at the operas for about 10 per cent less than the normal price.

Handel wrote to his brother-in-law, Michaelsen, from Venice in March 1729, promising to visit him in Halle in July.[13] He managed to engage five Italian singers, among them the male soprano Bernacchi, who had sung for him many years before in *Amadigi*, and a new first woman, Anna Strada, who was to be his leading soprano and faithful friend for the next seven years. With them was a powerful bass, Giovanni Riemschneider, from Hamburg. In all the singers were offered about £4,000, the total amount that Handel had been authorized to spend.

His business in Italy finished, Handel was able to visit Halle in June, earlier than he had expected, and to see his mother, who was now nearly eighty years old and blind. It was to be for the last time as she died less than two years later.

By July Handel was back in London, soon followed by his singers. His first action when they arrived was to arrange a private concert for the King at Kensington Palace. His Majesty, delighted with the performance, renewed his subscription of £1,000 a year to the Opera. Handel sat down to write *Lotario* for the revived Academy and the new venture commenced in December with ten performances of it. He followed this with *Parthenope* in the following February, using repeat performances of *Giulio Cesare* and *Tolomeo* as a stop-gap for the remainder of the season. Strada was a great success.

Disappointed with the financial returns from the 1729/30 season, the new Academy decided to re-engage Senesino. Somehow, he and Handel managed to settle their differences sufficiently to work together for the next three years and the operas *Poro*, *Ezio*, *Sosarme* and *Orlando* were produced and favourably received.

It was at this time that Handel's mind was turned to other kinds of music, prompted perhaps by certain outside events. There was an annual charitable performance in St Paul's – the Festival of the Sons of the Clergy – at which a Te Deum by Purcell was usually sung. In 1732 the organizers chose Handel's *Utrecht Te Deum* and *Jubilate* in its place, with two of the *Coronation Anthems*. This resulted in a total collection of £1,080 as against £718 for the previous year. Handel, no doubt, noted this with satisfaction and interest.

On Handel's birthday, Bernard Gates, Master of the children of the Chapel Royal, arranged a performance of *Esther* at the Music Club at the Crown and Anchor Tavern. This was repeated on 3 and 5 March. The success of this prompted an unauthorized performance at the Great Room in Villars Street in April.

Gates' *Esther* was given as a stage performance of a religious opera and no doubt it was in this form, as *Hamon and Mordecai*, that it was first produced in 1720 for the Duke of Chandos.[22] Handel's reply to the pirate version in Villars Street was to prepare a bigger and better version under his own direction. But meanwhile the Bishop of London, who was also Dean of the Chapel Royal, forbade the children to take part in further dramatic performances, though he raised no objections to the work being sung without action. A few days later Handel's own advertisement appeared: '*The Sacred Story* of ESTHER . . . N.B. There will be no Action on the Stage, but the House will be fitted up in a decent Manner, for the Audience.' Although Handel accepted the Bishop's edict and set the pattern for nearly all oratorio performances up to the present day, he still did his best to retain their dramatic atmosphere. In his own scores and the printed libretti stage directions such as 'Exit' and 'Exeunt' abound, and such notes as 'Athalia starting out of a slumber', or 'Samson blind and in chains' make it clear that Handel intended his singers somehow to make these things clear to the audience, however static the performance.

In several ways, however, the Bishop's veto worked out to Handel's advantage. A concert version with the use of music books made it easier for him to include more numerous and attractive choruses. These as Burney tells us,[18] largely replaced his former need of expensive first-class soloists. He was also able to use Wednesdays and Fridays in Lent, when stage plays were forbidden, and to enjoy a direct reduction in house charges. There is evidence[6] that £198 was saved in this way in 1736.

With all this in mind he wrote an oratorio *Deborah* which was performed in March 1733. He made the grave mistake of doubling his theatre prices. This cost him the goodwill of the public who proceeded to link his name with that of Sir Robert Walpole, who was at the time trying to force an unpopular tobacco Excise Bill through Parliament.

This was followed in May by a serious and final breach with Senesino. In the meantime the composer had accepted an invitation to visit Oxford with his singers and musicians to take part in a Public Act. Handel spent a profitable week there in July with daily performances of church music and oratorios, notably a new one called *Athalia*. His principal bass singer at this time was Gustavus Waltz, also a violoncellist who has been thought from a chance remark of Handel's to have been also his cook. (See: *Concerning Handel* by William C. Smith).

Returning to London to prepare for a new opera season in the winter, Handel found that a section of the nobility had leased the theatre in Lincoln's Inn Fields. They were making preparations to open in December with a rival opera *Ariadne*, set to music by Porpora and had engaged Senesino and three of Handel's former singers for the cast. Handel managed to replace Senesino with Giovanni Carestino, another castrato with a fine alto voice, and with Strada and Durastanti, who had remained loyal to him, re-opened his theatre on 30 October with a pasticcio-opera *Semiramis*.

These pasticcios were popular with London audiences and consisted of a selection of songs from recent operas, often by different composers. They were linked together by the arranger with recitatives of his own composition. In all, there are about ten of these concoctions associated with Handel. This was followed by a revival of *Ottone* and then by a new and better *Arianna*, set by Handel himself – a characteristic gesture. This received instant success, was twice attended by the Court and ran for seventeen performances.

By this time something like open war had broken out between the rival opera groups and sarcastic and scurrilous pamphlets were freely published. The Nobility took the further step of engaging Cuzzoni to sing for them against Handel. Fortunately he still retained Royal favour and consolidated this with a performance of *Parnasso in Festa*, written in honour of the wedding of Princess Anne

A page from the autograph score of Messiah

I give and bequeath to my Cousin Christian Gottlieb Handel of Coppenhagen one hundred Pounds sterl:

Item I give and bequeath to my Cousin Magister Christian August Roth of Halle in Saxony one hundred Pounds sterl:

Item I give and bequeath to my Cousin the Widow of George Taust, Pastor of giebichenstein near Halle in Saxony three hundred Pounds sterl:

And to Her six Children each two hundred Pounds sterl: All the next and residue of my Estate in ~~South sea~~ Bank Annuity's ~~Annuitys~~ or of whatsoever Kind or Nature, I give and bequeath unto my Dear Niece Johanna Friderica Floerken of Gotha in Saxony (born Michaelsen in Halle) whom I make my Sole Exec:rix of this my last Will

. In wittness Whereof I have hereunto set my hand this 1 Day of June 1750

George Frideric Handel

A page from Handel's will of 1750

with the Prince of Orange on 14 March 1734.

After this till mid-July, when Handel's contract with Heidegger finally expired, a number of earlier works such as *Sosarme*, *Acis* and *Pastor Fido* were revived, with frequent performances but often playing to nearly empty houses. The limited audience available for the two opera houses was far from sufficient to meet the heavy expense of the productions. As an example, Heidegger, who leased the King's Theatre to the Nobility for the coming season, produced figures to show that 'the undertakers must receive seventy-six thousand odd hundred pounds to bear their charges, before they become gainers.'[14]

Handel did his best. He went into partnership with John Rich and leased his new opera house at Covent Garden for the next four years. Rich was an eccentric character, once the most famous Harlequin of his time, but in later life living in seclusion, refusing interviews and surrounded by twenty-seven cats. Handel persuaded the King to give his annual opera grant of £1,000 directly to him and not to the Academy. He then opened his season with a new opera *Ariodante*, preceded by revivals of *Pastor Fido* and *Arianna*. As an added attraction for the first opera he introduced a ballet called *Terpsichore*, with his good friend Marie Sallé as chief danseuse, and reduced the gallery prices to 2s 6d. Similar ballets were written into the other operas, much to the advancement of their popularity. But unfortunately for Handel, the Prince of Wales became on increasingly bad terms with his father George II, who with his daughter, the Princess Royal, remained loyal Handelians. It was reported in 1734 that they 'sat freezing constantly at his empty Haymarket Opera, whilst the Prince with all the chief of the nobility went as constantly to that of Lincoln's Inn Fields'.[15]

Despite the report in 1735 that Handel's loss for the past two seasons was reputed 'at a great sum' he continued to pour out some of his finest works, notably *Alcina* in April which ran for eighteen performances. Then came a bitter attack against Mlle Sallé, based on her appearance in male attire as Cupid in *Alcina*. It led to her being hissed in public and to her retirement from Handel's cast. In July, too, Carestini left him for good.

*   *   *

Handel very sensibly decided to take a holiday. Despite his massive figure and robust health he was often concerned about himself. Many of his holidays were spent at spas and this time he went to Tunbridge Wells where he took the waters, probably as an antidote to the large quantity of food and drink which he found helpful to his energy and inspiration. There is indeed an apocryphal story about his visit to a country inn where he sat down and ordered dinner for three. There was some delay. Banging the table he enquired the reason. 'Sir', said the waiter, 'you ordered dinner for three, where are the company?' 'Bring up the dinner prestissimo' replied Handel, 'I am the company'. There still exists on the back of one of his music manuscripts the note: '12 Gallons Port, 12 bottles French', which suggests that occasional spa treatment may have had its place.

On his return to London he attended at least one performance of the rival opera. Lord Hervey wrote: 'Handel sat in great eminence and great pride in the middle of the pit, and seemed in silent triumph to insult this poor dying Opera in its agonies'.

Deciding on a spring season Handel staged no operas in the winter of 1735–36 and opened instead on 19 February 1736 with his fine setting of Dryden's *Alexander's Feast*. This drew a packed house and among the more popular items were the performances of instrumental concertos in and between the acts, with an organ concerto inserted just before the final chorus. John Beard, a new tenor, and Strada were the principal singers. Although Handel always retained a preference for the castrato voice, these singers were losing favour with the public, who regarded them as foreign spies and not infrequently accused them of being 'Jesuits in disguise'.

John Walsh the elder died on 13 March, the business passing to his younger son, who paid Handel £105 for a manuscript of *Alexander's Feast*. This he published practically in full with all the choruses – a very rare event. He also included the fine cantata *Cecilia Volgi* which Handel had inserted as an entracte.

After four repeat performances, together with two each of *Acis* and *Esther*, Handel arranged a short opera season in honour of the Prince of Wales' forthcoming marriage to the Princess of Saxe-Gotha. He wrote a new opera *Atalanta* for this and an anthem for the wedding itself. It is evident that he was now back in the Prince's favour and later it was his custom to hold some rehearsals and concerts at Carlton House, the Prince's official residence. Burney[16] tells us that if he was disturbed by the audience he would become violent and swear, despite the presence of the royal couple, though his rages were short-lived. There is a story about some wag untuning all the instruments of his orchestra just before a concert. After the first horrible discord he hurled a kettledrum at the leader of the orchestra, losing his huge white wig in the process.

Handel's next task, in August 1736 was the opera *Giustino*. During its composition he wrote a letter to his brother-in-law Michael Michaelsen, giving his approval for his niece Johanna to marry a Dr Johann Flörcke, professor of law at Halle University. He described her as his nearest relative and said that he had always loved her particularly. With the letter he sent a gold watch to the bridegroom and a solitaire diamond ring to his niece, its large stone weighing over $7\frac{1}{2}$ grains.

Giustino seems to have given Handel some trouble for he broke off its composition in September to begin writing his next opera *Arminio*. Completing this in less than a month, he had a final burst of energy and finished *Giustino* a week later. Both operas went on at Covent Garden early in 1737 with moderate success and against great opposition from the opera of the Nobility who had engaged the famous castrato Farinelli – the finest singer in Europe – as their star attraction.

Handel, no doubt expecting privileged treatment, went on staging his new opera in Lent, using the forbidden Wednesdays and Fridays. This was soon stopped by the Lord Chamberlain who, in a letter dated 3 March to all London theatre managers, renewed the existing ban on all such performances. To honour his contract with John Rich, Handel reverted to oratorios, starting with two performances of his serenata *Il Parnasso in Festa*, a work which required no action. After that he completed the season with ten performances of *Alexander's Feast*, a fresh edition of *Il Trionfo del Tempo* and *Esther*.

But work and frustration combined to overtax Handel and the strain was beginning to tell on him both mentally and physically. A press report in April spoke of him recovering from rheumatism and hoped that he would be able to accompany the next performance of *Giustino*. But on 14 May the *London Evening Post* had worse news: 'The ingenious Mr Handell is very much indispos'd, and it's thought with a Pareletick Disorder, he having at present no Use of his Right Hand, which, if he don't regain, the Publick will be depriv'd of his fine Compositions.'

Handel, very sensibly, handed his commitments over to someone else, including the production of his new opera *Berenice*, whose minuet still retains an eternal attraction for most music lovers. The someone else was most likely John Christopher Smith the younger, Handel's music pupil, who in 1732 had appeared in his own right as a composer and director of operas at Covent Garden. Handel made his way to the spa of Aix-la-Chapelle, where we are told that he had 'recourse to the vapour baths . . . over which he sat near three times as long as hath ever been the practice. Whoever knows anything of the nature of these baths will, from this instance, form some idea of his surprising constitution. His sweats were profuse beyond what can well be imagined. His cure, from the manner as well as from the quickness with which it was wrought, passed with the Nuns for a miracle. When, but a few hours from the time of his quitting the bath, they heard him at the organ of the principal church as well as convent, playing in a manner so much beyond any they had ever been used to, such a conclusion in such persons was natural enough'.

Some later biographers have remarked cynically that the good nuns must have found it difficult to equate this miracle with Handel's heretical background. Whatever the spiritual background, the good nuns and their treatment lasted Handel well for the next eight years. They were years of hardship, frustration and physical discomfort. We have noted that till now, when he was fifty-two years of age, there is no record of his missing a rehearsal or performance.

* * *

On his return to England, Handel found another sad blow awaiting him. His friend and protector, Queen Caroline of Anspach, was dying. On 7 December George II ordered him to write a funeral anthem for her. In the space of ten days the *Ways of Zion*, the noblest funeral anthem of all time, was written, rehearsed and sung in Westminster Abbey on 17 December. The anthem drew high praise, the performance itself, with such brief rehearsal, rather less. One hundred and eighty vocal and instrumental performers took part.

Anticipating the end of Royal mourning, Handel began the composition of his next opera *Faramondo*, to be staged in January 1738, and shortly afterwards Fate had better things in store for him. John Walsh put out a magnificent edition of *Alexander's Feast*, followed by a fine engraved portrait of the composer. Every member of the Royal family subscribed to it and Jonathan Tyers, the proprietor of Vauxhall Gardens erected, at his own expense, a fine marble statue, costing £300, to his honour. The elegant engraving of Handel, above a scene depicting *Alexander's Feast*, by Houbraken, the celebrated Dutch artist, was distributed free to all subscribers to the music volume.

Shortly before this time, Charles Jennens, a wealthy manufacturer and patron of the Arts, had offered to Handel the libretto of an oratorio called *Saul*. Handel began his setting of this work about July 1738, but not till he had written and produced his mildly comic opera *Serse*. The first aria in this work 'Ombra mai fu' has been known ever since as the immortal 'Largo', though in real fact it is scored 'Larghetto e piano' and is concerned with the hero sleeping off too much lunch underneath a tree. This opera, which is packed with beautiful arias, was, shamefully, a failure. Handel turned to instrumental music. In close collaboration with the younger Walsh, he assembled a set of six organ concertos, his Opus 4, together with their instrumental parts. Improved relations are evident from the copperplate inscription on the title page: '*These Six Concertos were Publish'd by Mr Walsh from my own copy Corrected by my Self, and to Him only I have given my Right therein, George Frideric Handel.*'

If this dedication cost Handel any pride he was amply repaid by the popularity of this and subsequent editions. Indeed Burney wrote of them: 'Public players on keyed instruments, as well as private, totally subsisted on these concertos for near thirty years'. Walsh followed up his good fortune by extracting from the composer a set of seven trio sonatas and twelve concerti grossi, the actual interval music which Handel was using himself between the acts of his performances.

Saul was sung in January 1739 and had six performances. A feature of the accompaniment was a specially designed carillon, about which Jennens wrote: 'Mr Handel's head is more full of maggots than ever. I found yesterday in his room a very queer instrument . . . some call it a Tubalcain. 'Tis played upon with keys like a Harpsichord and with this Cyclopean instrument he designs to make poor Saul stark mad'.[4]

Saul was followed by *Israel in Egypt*, a failure with only three performances. It is now evident that this great work, with its massive choruses, so popular with any competent choral society, was long before its time.

Handel always had a great respect for St Cecilia, the patron saint of music. He wrote a special Ode for her feast day, 22 November 1739 and preceded it with *Alexander's Feast*, a work also written in her honour. His courtesy to the Saint received an ill award, for the winter of 1739 was the most severe in living memory. The Thames froze over, oxen were roasted on the ice and theatre performances almost came to a standstill. As the cold increased, Handel, with only a handful of singers in his company, led by Francesina and John Beard, limited most concerts to the simpler oratorios and cantatas which demanded no more than soprano, tenor and bass voices. Among these was his newly written *L'Allegro ed Il Penseroso*, arranged by Jennens from Milton's two poems, with a composition of his own called *Il Moderato* tacked on as a third part.

Handel returned to Italian opera for his 1741 season, but it was to be for the last time. Despite the beauties of *Imeneo* and *Deidamia*, both were failures. Enemies, notably a Lady Brown, arranged social events to clash with his performances and we read in the contemporary papers of 'little Vermin, who . . . pull down even his Bills as fast as he has them pasted up'. There is, too, a letter from an admirer who wrote sadly: 'this Oratorio (*L'Allegro*) on Wednesday next is . . . probably the last for ever in this Country'. This was probably Handel's darkest hour and both he and his friends must have thought that he was facing impossible odds and the end of his career in England.

Then came a most timely invitation from the Lord Lieutenant of Ireland for Handel to visit Dublin and to give there a series of subscription concerts. It is said that there was also an agreement for him to write a special piece of music to be performed in aid of Dublin's three main charities. Either for this purpose, or by a happy chance, he had been provided by Charles Jennens with the libretto of *Messiah*. This he set to music in three weeks at the end of August. In a further burst of inspiration he followed this with *Samson*, a much more heavily scored work. Then taking *Messiah* and seven of his earlier works with him he set off for Dublin in November, probably accompanied by the faithful Smith.

Handel's stay in Dublin was an unqualified success and he wrote happily to Jennens about the 'Politeness of this generous Nation'. A new coloratura singer, Signora Avoglio, whom he must have engaged in London, followed him to Ireland. She may well have sung in the last set of Italian chamber duets he wrote in the previous summer, four excerpts from which were used in the composition of *Messiah*. In his letter, he wrote that she 'pleases extraordinary'. Susanna Cibber, who had left her unpleasant husband, and was with a touring theatrical company in Dublin also joined his cast. She made her name immortal in the first performance of *Messiah* on 13 April 1742 in the Musick Hall in Fishamble Street.

* * *

Refreshed in spirit and with his finances restored, Handel returned to England in Mid-August 1742. He found the opera of the Nobility bankrupt and in a state of chaos. Handel arranged an oratorio season early in 1743, starting with *Samson* and including Signora Avoglio and Mrs Cibber among the singers.

The fickle public, tired of bad opera, decided to support the oratorios, except *Messiah*, which aroused religious prejudice, so that Handel ended his season with a handsome profit. Meanwhile George II in person was leading a British Army against the French to victory at Dettingen.

Before his return Handel had completed a magnificent *Te Deum* and an anthem which were performed at the Chapel Royal in September 1743. But as his stock rose with the King, he managed to fall out with the Prince of Wales, and more sadly still with his friend and secretary, the elder Smith.

1744 produced another oratorio season with *Semele*, really an opera, being slipped in without action, together with *Joseph*, another new work, set to a libretto by James Miller. Revivals of *Samson* and *Saul* completed the repertoire. In the provinces, oratorio began to take hold. *Alexander's Feast* was performed at Ruckholt House in Essex. Meanwhile Handel received from Jennens the libretto of *Belshazzar*, the length of which caused him some embarrassment. The problem was tactfully solved by printing the text in full in the programmes with the note: 'N.B. The *Oratorio* being thought too long, several things are Mark'd with a black Line drawn down the Margin as omitted in the performance'.

Emboldened by the success of his twelve concerts in the Spring of 1744, Handel started a longer series of twenty-four in the autumn with *Belshazzar* and *Hercules* as new attractions for the beginning of 1745. Whether Handel had offended still more of the nobility is not recorded. But his audiences shrank to such small numbers that he felt it necessary to publish an apologetic letter in the papers offering to refund subscriptions 'before my losses become too great to support'. Strain and frustration took their toll of his health and though his subscribers publicly refused to reclaim their subscriptions, his season drew to an end in April with *Messiah*, like the rest of the oratorios, played to almost empty houses. Charles Jennens, we may now think presumptuously, may have blamed Handel for this. In August 1745 he wrote to a friend: 'I shall show you a collection I gave Handel, call'd *Messiah*, which I value highly, and he has made a fine Entertainment of it, tho' not near so good as he might and ought to have done'.

Handel took a prolonged holiday. He stayed with Lord Gainsborough in Rutland[17] and went on to the spa at Scarborough to recuperate, returning to London in October. In this month the Earl of Shaftesbury wrote to his cousin James Harris, 'Poor Handel looks something better. I hope he will entirely recover in due time, though he has been a good deal disordered in his head'. Threats of a Jacobite invasion, after the Young Pretender had landed in Scotland in mid-July, made an autumn season impossible and by December London was in a panic stricken state. Handel's two contributions were a *Song for the Gentlemen Volunteers of the City of London*, followed by another song *From Scourging Rebellion* as the retreat of the Young Pretender and his army on Christmas Day, 1745 changed the whole picture. Handel, farseeing as usual, anticipated his final defeat at Culloden in April 1746, and wrote his *Occasional Oratorio* in honour of the Duke of Cumberland for performance on 14 February 1746.

More letters from the 4th Earl of Shaftesbury to his cousin James Harris have recently been found[23] and give us important details. The first, whose date I have corrected to 1746, begins: 'London 23 February. Handel call'd on me this morning, his spirit and genious are astonishing. He rather gets than loses by his Houses. However, as he has obliged his former subscribers without detriment to himself he is contented. Next Wednesday is his last of performing this season. This new composition [the *Occasional Oratorio*] is indeed excellent.'

After Culloden, Handel sat down to write a full-scale oratorio in praise of the Duke of Cumberland, thinly disguised as *Judas Maccabaeus*, an Old Testament hero who had saved his countrymen with numerous battles against the foe. Actually, performance of *Judas* was delayed till April 1747 although Handel finished its composition on 11 August 1746.

Lord Shaftesbury wrote happily from London[23]: '20 January 1747. Mr Handel call'd on me tother day. He is now in perfect health and I really think grown young again. There is a most absurd and ridiculous opera going forward at present and as it is not likely to meet with success he is delighted.' The opera in question was *Phaeton* by Paradies, a composer who had recently arrived in England.

Judas Maccabaeus tapped a new audience, the London Jews, who flocked to see their Old Testament hero triumphant. The librettist, Thomas Morell, received a present from the Duke of Cumberland. Both immediately and for the remainder of the composer's life, this martial oratorio enjoyed very great popularity. From now onwards, Handel decided to concentrate on oratorio seasons in Lent and, with his profitable Jewish audiences in mind, wrote *Joshua* and *Alexander Balus* for his 1748 season. Morell's libretti, as with so many sequels, lacked inspiration. *Joshua* was a relative success, *Alexander Balus* less so. Both oratorios, however, contain many beautiful and richly scored numbers worthy of revival to-day. One of the successful numbers from *Joshua*, 'See the conquering hero comes' was promptly incorporated by Handel into the next performance of *Judas Maccabaeus*.

Recent evidence[23] tells us how closely the copyright of these oratorios was safeguarded by Smith and Handel. Some obligation was imposed on the use of library scores made for friends and patrons. Lord Shaftesbury refused a request from Dr Hayes of Oxford to borrow his copy of *Joshua* with the reply: 'As to Joshua, I believe Mr Handel will not chuse to have it perform'd at Oxford or anywhere but by himself.' But later, Dr Hayes received the score with this note: 'Smyth has been with me just now to say, there is no objection to my lending the score of Joshua to Dr Hayes, yet this is done under a confidence of Dr Hayes' honour that he will not suffer any copy to be taken or to get about from his having been in possession of the score. For otherwise both Handel and Smyth (his copiest) will be injur'd.'

In 1749 Handel produced a new oratorio *Susanna* – we might fairly describe it as a biblical light opera. We quote Lord Shaftesbury again[23]: 'I hear *Susanna* much commended by some who heard Galli and Frasi's parts. I understand there are no less than seven parts in this that I fear the lower ones will go off bad enough, but this is by the by.' In the same letter: 'The old Buck is excessively healthy and full of spirits. He says he saw my cousin Thos. Harris the day before he left town who can tell all about him and his designs.'

Susanna played to a full house and his next design was *Solomon*, an impressive scriptural work with the famous judgement scene as its core. By now, from sheer merit, Handel had become a national asset, despite his independence of character. There is an excellent example of this in the correspondence about the *Royal Fireworks Music*, his next popular composition to celebrate the Peace of Aix-la-Chapelle. In his wishes to include violins and not to have the dress rehearsal in Vauxhall Gardens, Handel defied the King himself, though he was forced to give in about the last point. When the rehearsal took place on 22 April it caused a traffic jam on London Bridge, then the only roadway over the Thames, and something like a local riot in Vauxhall Gardens. Although the real event on 27 April in St James's Park was a partial fiasco through a premature fire at the display, the music, with its rich scoring for brass instruments, achieved an instant and lasting popularity.

Handel took a special interest in the Foundling Hospital, newly built in Lamb's Conduit Fields, and arranged a special programme of music for the opening of its chapel in May 1749, containing excerpts from *Solomon*, the *Fireworks Music* and a new *Foundling Anthem*, partly made from the *Ways of Zion*. He followed this with the generous gift of an organ for the Chapel, ordered from Dr Jonathan Morse, of Barnet. Then he left for a short holiday in Bath with his friend James Quin, the actor, and accompanied

44

by the elder J. C. Smith, their differences, one hopes, being settled. In the meantime he had written his new oratorio *Theodora* for use in the 1750 season. Although he thought highly of it, it attracted poor audiences. His own explanation was: 'The Jews will not come to it because it is a Christian story, and the ladies will not come, because it is a virtuous one'. Another composition, *Alceste*, written for Rich, for some reason never reached production, so Handel, with commendable economy re-used its music for a bright little entracte called the *Choice of Hercules*.

After many years a new and fine castrato voice was heard again in London, one Gaetano Guadagni. Despite Burney's description of him as 'a wild and careless singer',[18] Handel promptly re-wrote several arias in *Messiah* for him and gave two performances of this work in the Foundling Hospital Chapel to open his new organ. It is important to note that *Messiah*, whose repeated performances brought in nearly £7,000 for this charity in Handel's lifetime, was the one and only oratorio he ever performed in a church.

From now on the work increased in popularity and Handel customarily used it to end every oratorio season. The Foundling Hospital, in gratitude made him a Governor. Handel, not to be outdone in generosity, made them a bequest in his Will of a full score of *Messiah*, with a set of parts, which may still be seen to-day among their archives.

In August 1750 a press report said that: 'Mr Handel, who went to Germany to visit his friends some Time since, and between the Hague and Haarlem had the Misfortune to be overturned, by which he was terribly hurt, is now out of Danger'. But, by December, Handel was in good health and writing to his old friend Telemann to send him a collection of exotic plants.

* * *

On 13 February 1751, mid-way through the composition of *Jephtha*, one of his finest works, Handel's sight failed him.

There is a pathetic note in German at the foot of page 182 of the autograph: 'Got as far as this on Wednesday . . . unable to go on owing to weakening of the sight of my left eye'. It is significant that this occurred in the great chorus: 'How dark O Lord are Thy decrees, all hid from mortal sight.' Although he is thought only to have lost the sight of one eye, the tails of the notes in the string parts are left uncompleted. But on his birthday, 23 February, his sight improved enough to resume work and he added a little footnote to this effect on the next page. It was not till 30 August that he completed his manuscript. This was his last new work, though he made alterations and additions to other oratorios, notably *Judas Maccabaeus* and *Esther* during the following years, together with an English version of *Il Trionfo* as *The Triumph of Time and Truth* in 1757.

When his sight failed, his first action was to send for the younger John Christopher Smith who was then abroad. From his prompt arrival till the time of Handel's death, the younger Smith gave him all possible support and help.

Lord Shaftesbury wrote twice[23] to report the composer's continued good health despite his eye trouble. The last letter, dated 28 March 1751, is almost frivolous: 'As to Harmony here, that is over for the season, but the Buck is now so well that I much hope it will flourish yet another year in renewed vigour.'

In June, Handel revisited Bath, with a 'Mr Smith' in attendance. He returned to London to be examined by Samuel Sharp, surgeon to Guy's Hospital. Sharp told him that he had 'Gutta Serena', probably the disease we know today as glaucoma. Sir John Hawkins tells us that: 'from the moment this opinion of his case was communicated to him, his spirits forsook him; and that fortitude which had supported him under affliction of another kind, deserted him *upon being told* that a freedom of pain in the visual organs was all that he had to hope for, the remainder of his days'.[19]

On 3 November 1752, Handel was operated upon for cataract by William Bromfield, Surgeon to the Princess of Wales, with temporary benefit. There is a contemporary note that he was 'able to go abroad' (i.e. out-of-doors) though this improvement did not last. He was also operated on by the notorious Chevalier Taylor – usually regarded as a perambulating quack – either before or after Bromfield's intervention, or perhaps both. An anonymous poem was published on 15 August 1758 claiming that Taylor had restored Handel's sight. But a later note by Taylor himself said that: 'upon drawing the curtain we found the bottom defective from a paralytic disorder.' The four codicils to Handel's Will, dated 1756, 1757 and 1759 all show evidence of very defective sight – if any. Yet other evidence suggests that at times, especially in 1754,[20] he could see sufficiently to make notes in his music scores. Whether blind or not he continued to accompany his oratorios and to play organ concertos, when his health permitted, up to a week before his death.

Two final excerpts from the Shaftesbury letters give us good news for 1757.[23] On 8 February: 'Mr Handel is better than he has been for some years and finds he can compose Chorus's as well as other music to his own (and consequently to the hearer's) satisfaction. His memory is strengthened of late to an astonishing degree. This intelligence must give you pleasure.' And again on 31 December: '. . . I saw Mr Handel the other day who is pretty well and had just finished the composing of several new songs for Frederica his new singer, from whom he has great expectations.' Cassandra Frederick, aged 15, who had been something of a child prodigy on the harpsichord, sang for Handel in his oratorios during 1758. Her success may be judged by the fact that John Walsh published a number of these new songs under her name five years after Handel's death.

His last public appearance was at a performance of *Messiah* on 6 April 1759, the last of his concert series, after which he collapsed and was taken to his house in Brook Street. There he died, conscious to the last, on the morning of 14 April. Reports tell us that he had been for some time past in a bad state of health and had planned to visit Bath on 7 April to take the waters there, though in the event he was too ill to make the journey.

It is sad to relate that he quarrelled again with the elder Smith in Tunbridge Wells a year or two before his death, but through the good offices of the son they were re-united and the faithful secretary became heir to a large sum of money and all Handel's music books and manu-scripts. This included his large harpsichord and an organ. All these effects Smith carefully preserved and left to his son when he died in January 1763. Handel made many bequests to his personal friends, including one of a thousand pounds to the Decayed Musicians' Fund. This is now the Royal Society of Musicians. The residue of his estate, which including the above bequests totalled about £20,000, passed to his niece Johanna Flörcke in Halle.

At his own request, noted in the last codicil to his Will, Handel was buried in Westminster Abbey. His funeral was attended by about 3,000 people and later, above his tomb in Poet's Corner, there was erected a fine marble memorial by Roubiliac.

So passed a great man, who by personal integrity, hard work and genius achieved the respect and affection of his contemporaries and who left behind him music which has become immortal. In life he was kind, just and charitable in his dealing with others. Though at times hot tempered, he was never vindictive, even against those who attacked him. Beethoven, Gluck and Mozart in turn spoke glowing tributes to him in their own time. But perhaps the finest epitaph came from Haydn, who, standing by his tomb in Westminster Abbey, said with deep emotion: 'Truly he is the father of us all'.[21]

REFERENCES

(1) ROBINSON, PERCY   *Handel and His Orbit*. London 1908

(2) MAINWARING, J.   *Memoirs of the late G. F. Handel.* London 1760

(3) HALL, JAMES S.   'The Problem of Handel's Latin Church Music.' *Musical Times.* London, April 1959

(4) FLOWER, SIR NEWMAN   *George Frideric Handel*. London 1959

(5) HALL, JAMES S.   'Handel among the Carmelites.' *Dublin Review.* Summer 1959

(6) SMITH, WILLIAM C.   *Concerning Handel*. London 1948

(7) SMITH, WILLIAM C.   'Handel's First Song on the London Stage.' *Music & Letters.* October 1935

(8) DENT, EDWARD J.   *Handel* (Great Lives). London 1934

(9) COLMAN, FRANCIS   '*Opera-Registers from 1712–34.*' Edited by Konrad Sasse. Händel Jahrbuch. Leipzig 1959

(10) HEIRONS, Dr R.   *Journal of the History of Medicine and Allied Sciences.* London 1952. Vol. VII, No. 4

(11) YOUNG, PERCY M.   *Handel* (Master Musicians). London 1947

(12) HALL, JAMES S.   'John Christopher Smith, Handel's Friend and Secretary.' *Musical Times.* London, March 1955

(13) MÜLLER, E. H.   *The Letters & Writings of George Frideric Handel*. London 1935

(14) DEUTSCH, OTTO E.   *Handel: A Documentary Biography* London 1955

(15) STREATFEILD, R. A.   *Handel*. London 1909

(16) BURNEY, CHARLES   *Commemoration of Handel*. London 1785

(17) MATTHEWS, BETTY   'Unpublished Letters concerning Handel.' *Music & Letters.* July 1959

(18) BURNEY, CHARLES   *A General History of Music.* London 1776–89

(19) HAWKINS, SIR JOHN   *A General History of the Science and Practice of Music.* London 1776

(20) HALL, JAMES S.   'Mr Handel, his health.' *St Mary's Hospital Gazette.* London, April/May 1960

(21) SCHOELCHER, V.   *The Life of Handel.* London 1857

(22) DEAN, WINTON   *Handel's Dramatic Oratorios and Masques.* London 1959

(23) MATTHEWS, BETTY   Handel – More unpublished Letters. *Music & Letters,* April 1961